THIS BOOK
BELONGS TO

_____
_____
_____

WOMEN

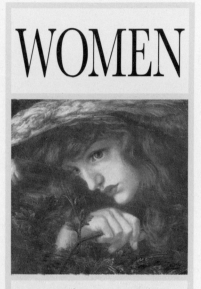

IN WORDS AND PICTURES

JARROLD
PUBLISHING

WOMEN

A woman is the full circle. Within her is the power to create, nurture and transform. A woman knows nothing can come to fruition without light.

DIANE MARIECHILD

If men are always more or less deceived on the subject of women, it is because they forget that they and women do not speak altogether the same language.

HENRI AMIEL

We women do talk too much, but even then we don't tell half we know.

LADY NANCY ASTOR

WOMEN

PORTRAIT OF WOMAN WITH WHITE JABOT
Pierre-Auguste Renoir 1841–1919

WOMEN

FLAMING JUNE
Frederic Leighton 1830–1896

WOMEN

The average man is more interested in a woman who is interested in him than he is in a woman – any woman – with beautiful legs.

MARLENE DIETRICH

Women are like pictures, of no value in the hands of a fool, till he hears men of sense bid high for the purchase.

GEORGE FARQUHAR

Women forgive injuries, but never forget slights.

T.C. HALIBURTON [SAM SLICK]

WOMEN

As for the women,
though we scorn and flout 'em,
We may live with them, but
cannot live without 'em.

FREDERICK REYNOLDS

A woman's guess is
much more accurate
than a man's certainty.

RUDYARD KIPLING

Whether they give
or refuse, it delights
women to have been
asked.

OVID

Women as the
guardians of children
possess great power.
They are the moulders
of their children's
personalities and the
arbiters of their
development.

ANN OAKLEY

WOMEN

WOMAN WITH UMBRELLA
Claude Monet
1840–1926

WOMEN

PERDITA, *George Patten 1801–1865*

Whatever women do they must do twice as well as men to be thought half as good. Luckily, this is not difficult.

CHARLOTTE WHITTON

A woman without a laugh in her... is the greatest bore in existence.

WILLIAM MAKEPEACE THACKERAY

QUEEN FOR A DAY
Paul Falconer Poole 1807–1879

WOMEN

PEASANTS OUTSIDE CHURCH
Albert Edelfelt

WOMEN

Men play the game: women know the score.

ROGER WODDIS

There is only one political career for which women are perfectly suitable, diplomacy.

CLARE BOOTH LUCE

Women have more imagination than men. They need it to tell us how wonderful we are.

ARNOLD H. GLASGOW

WOMEN

To see her is to love her
And love but her for ever;
For Nature made her what she is,
And never made anither!

ROBERT BURNS

Any man who
thinks he is smarter
than his wife is
married to a very
smart woman.

The most precious
possession that ever
comes to a man in
this world is a
woman's heart.

J.G. HOLLAND

Man's work lasts
till set of sun;
Woman's work is
never done.

PICKING HYACINTHS, SPRINGTIME
Arthur Herbert Buckland fl. 1895–1927

WOMEN

THE LAST SUMMER DAYS
Thomas Brooks 1818–1891

WOMEN

In the years since I began following the ways of my grandmothers, I have come to value the teaching, stories and daily examples of living which they shared with me. I pity the younger girls of the future who will miss out on meeting some of these fine old women.

BEVERLY HUNGRY WOLF

WOMEN

When you educate a man you educate an individual; when you educate a woman you educate a whole family.

DR CHARLES D. McIVER

Without women – the beginning of our life would be deprived of assistance, the middle portion of pleasure, and the end of consolation.

VICTOR J.E. JOUY

Women are at last becoming persons first and wives second, and that is as it should be.

MAY SARTON

WOMEN

THE VISITATION
Hungarian School

LA GHIRLANDATA
Dante Gabriel Rossetti 1828–1882

WOMEN

If it was woman who put man out of Paradise, it is still woman, and woman only, who can lead him back.

ELBERT HUBBARD

There have been women in the past far more daring than we would need to be now, who ventured all and gained a little, but survived after all.

GERMAINE GREER

I have always said it: Nature meant woman to be her masterpiece.

GOTTHOLD LESSING

Woman is the salvation or destruction of the family. She carries its destinies in the folds of her mantle.

HENRI AMIEL

WOMEN

Because of their agelong training in human relations – for that is what feminine intuition really is – women have a special contribution to make to any group enterprise.

MARGARET MEAD

A woman who is loved always has success.

VICKI BAUM

A liberated woman is one who feels confident in herself, and is happy in what she is doing. She is a person who has a sense of self.... It all comes down to freedom of choice.

BETTY FORD

All I ask of a woman is that she feel gently towards me when my heart feels kindly towards her.

D.H. LAWRENCE

WOMEN

DAYDREAMS
Marcus Stone 1840-1921

WOMEN

A PRETTY PORTRAIT
George L. Seymour 1883–1916

WOMEN

They talk about a woman's sphere
As though it had a limit,
There's not a place in earth or heaven,
There's not a task to mankind given,
There's not a blessing or a woe
There's not a whispered "yes" or "no",
There's not a life or birth that has
A feather's weight of worth
Without a woman in it!

KATE FIELD

One is not born a
woman, one becomes
one.

SIMONE DE BEAUVOIR

Taking joy in life is a
woman's best cosmetic.

ROSALIND RUSSELL

If a woman is
sufficiently ambitious,
determined *and* gifted
– there is practically
nothing she can't do.

HELEN LAWRENSON

WOMEN

Women have always been the guardians of wisdom and humanity, which makes them natural, but usually secret, rulers. The time has come for them to rule openly, but together with and not against men.

CHARLOTTE WOLFF

The only time a woman really succeeds in changing a man is when he is a baby.

NATALIE WOOD

She openeth her mouth with wisdom; and in her tongue is the law of kindness.

THE BOOK OF PROVERBS

MISS DENE
Frederic Leighton 1830–1896

ALSO IN THIS SERIES

Cats — In Words and Pictures
Dogs — In Words and Pictures
Golf — In Words and Pictures

ALSO AVAILABLE

In Praise of Happiness
In Praise of Friends
In Praise of Mothers
In Praise of Children

First published in Great Britain in 1996 by
JARROLD PUBLISHING LTD
Whitefriars, Norwich NR3 1TR

Developed and produced by
FOUR SEASONS PUBLISHING LTD
1 Durrington Avenue, London SW20 8NT

Text research by *Pauline Burrett*
Designed in association with *The Bridgewater Book Company*
Edited by *David Notley* and *Peter Bridgewater*
Picture research by *Vanessa Fletcher*
Printed in Dubai

Copyright © 1996 Four Seasons Publishing Ltd

ISBN 0-7117-0870-3

ACKNOWLEDGEMENTS

Four Seasons Publishing Ltd would like to thank all those
who kindly gave permission to reproduce the words and visual
material in this book; copyright holders have been identified
where possible and we apologise for any inadvertent omissions.

We would particularly like to thank the following
for the use of pictures: *Bridgeman Art Library, e.t. archive,
Fine Art Photographic Library.*

Front Cover: IDLE MOMENTS, *Charles Edward Perugini* 1839–1918
Title Page: LA GHIRLANDATA, *Dante Gabriel Rossetti* 1828–1882
Endpaper: LIFE IN THE HAREM, *John Frederick Lewis*
Frontispiece: DAYDREAMING, *Dewey Bates* 1851–1899
Back Cover: THE LAST SUMMER DAYS, *Thomas Brooks* 1818–1891